Glide Through the Marshy Terrain of
ALLIGATORS &
CROCODILES

Published by Wildlife Education, Ltd.
12233 Thatcher Court, Poway, California 92064
contact us at: **1-800-477-5034**
e-mail us at: **animals@zoobooks.com**
visit us at: **www.zoobooks.com**

ISBN 1-932396-03-9

Alligators & Crocodiles

Created and Written by
John Bonnett Wexo

Scientific Consultants
James P. Bacon, Jr., Ph.D.
Curator of Reptiles
San Diego Zoo

John L. Behler
Curator of Reptiles
New York Zoological Park (Bronx Zoo)

Contents

Alligators and crocodiles have fascinated people for centuries. Many tall tales have been told about these giant reptiles with the long tails. They are the original models for many dragons, serpents, and other fairy tale monsters.

The true story of alligators and crocodiles is even more fascinating. The name "crocodile" was first used about 2,000 years ago by Greek adventurers who were traveling in Egypt. The huge crocodiles reminded them of a tiny lizard called "krokodeilos" that lived back in their Greek villages. So the world's biggest reptile got its name from one of the world's smallest. Alligators got their name in a similar way. Spanish adventurers exploring the coast of Florida gave them the name "el legarto," which means "the lizard."

There is one other animal very closely related to alligators and crocodiles. It is called a *gharial* (**gair-ee-uhl**). This word comes from India, where gharials live. It was so named because its head and snout resembled a long-necked Indian jar, or *ghara*. The gharial's jaws are extremely long and thin.

Together, alligators, crocodiles, and gharials make up the group of animals known as *crocodilians* (krok-uh-**dil**-ee-uhns). Crocodilians are the world's largest *reptiles*. A reptile is a cold-blooded animal that has scaly skin, lays eggs, and breathes with lungs. Crocodilians continue to grow throughout their lives. Some males grow to be more than 15 feet long. And they may weigh over 500 pounds. Females are usually smaller than the males.

There are also "dwarf" species of alligators and crocodiles that seldom get longer than four or five feet. And, of course, others can grow to gigantic sizes. A saltwater crocodile captured near the coast of India was reported to be 27½ feet long and weighed over 1,000 pounds.

No one knows exactly how old this crocodile was, but we do know that crocodilians can live a long time. An alligator in a zoo once lived for 56 years. Some scientists think that crocodiles living in the wild can live to be over 100 years old.

This young crocodile is trying to capture a frog, but doesn't seem to have the "hang" of it yet. But like all crocodilians, when it grows up, it will be an excellent hunter.

The body of a crocodilian is made for living on land and in water. Crocodiles, alligators, and gharials share many features that allow them to do this. They have legs and feet for walking on land, but they also have long, powerful tails for swimming.

Crocodilians are very strong animals. And besides that, a tough coat of "armor" covers their bodies. As a result, the adults have few natural enemies strong enough to harm them.

At first glance, all crocodilians may look alike. But there are many important differences between them, as you will see below.

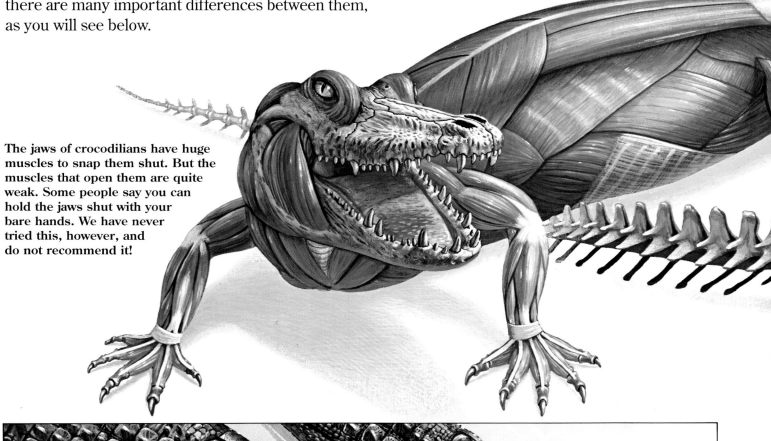

A crocodile's tail is longer than the rest of its body. And the strong tail muscles are used in many important ways. They supply the power for swimming by whipping the tail back and forth through the water.

The jaws of crocodilians have huge muscles to snap them shut. But the muscles that open them are quite weak. Some people say you can hold the jaws shut with your bare hands. We have never tried this, however, and do not recommend it!

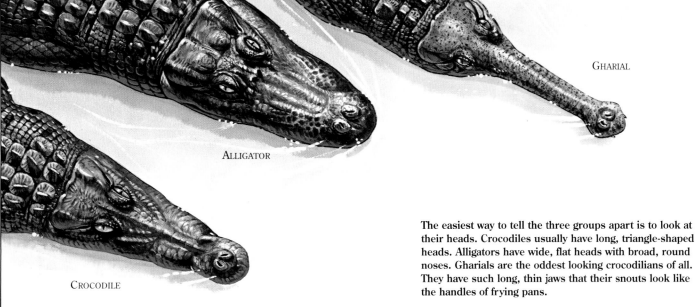

GHARIAL

ALLIGATOR

CROCODILE

The easiest way to tell the three groups apart is to look at their heads. Crocodiles usually have long, triangle-shaped heads. Alligators have wide, flat heads with broad, round noses. Gharials are the oddest looking crocodilians of all. They have such long, thin jaws that their snouts look like the handles of frying pans.

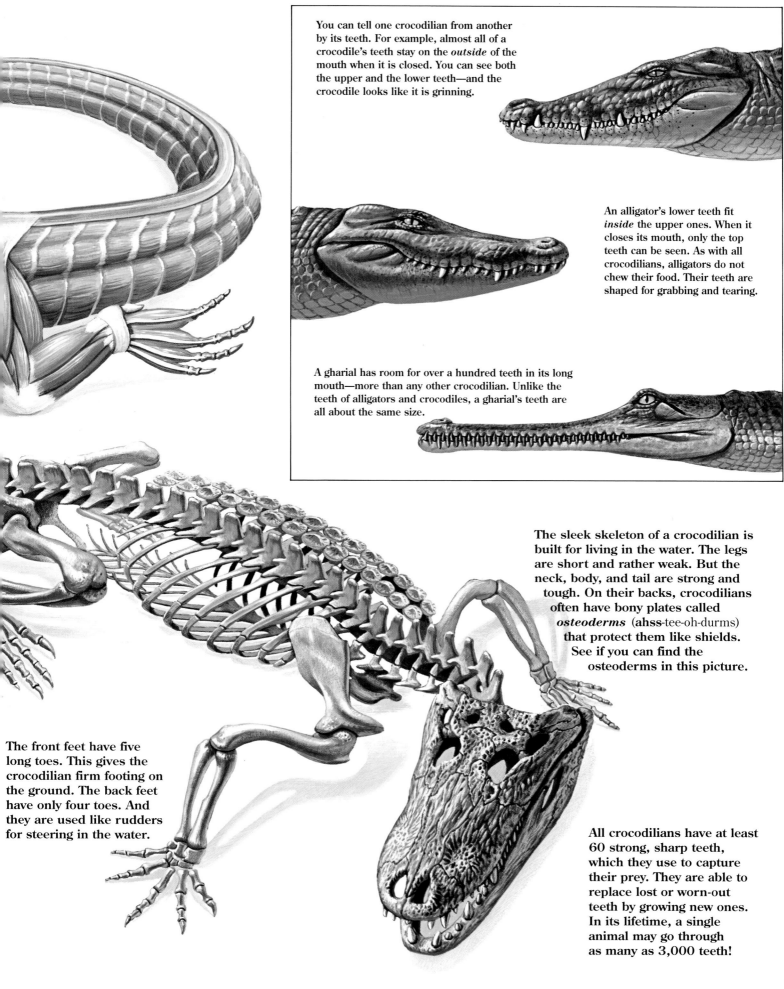

You can tell one crocodilian from another by its teeth. For example, almost all of a crocodile's teeth stay on the *outside* of the mouth when it is closed. You can see both the upper and the lower teeth—and the crocodile looks like it is grinning.

An alligator's lower teeth fit *inside* the upper ones. When it closes its mouth, only the top teeth can be seen. As with all crocodilians, alligators do not chew their food. Their teeth are shaped for grabbing and tearing.

A gharial has room for over a hundred teeth in its long mouth—more than any other crocodilian. Unlike the teeth of alligators and crocodiles, a gharial's teeth are all about the same size.

The sleek skeleton of a crocodilian is built for living in the water. The legs are short and rather weak. But the neck, body, and tail are strong and tough. On their backs, crocodilians often have bony plates called *osteoderms* (ahss-tee-oh-durms) that protect them like shields. See if you can find the osteoderms in this picture.

The front feet have five long toes. This gives the crocodilian firm footing on the ground. The back feet have only four toes. And they are used like rudders for steering in the water.

All crocodilians have at least 60 strong, sharp teeth, which they use to capture their prey. They are able to replace lost or worn-out teeth by growing new ones. In its lifetime, a single animal may go through as many as 3,000 teeth!

There are **21 kinds** (or species) of crocodilians in the world. Most of these are crocodiles. There is only one species of gharial, and only two species that are called alligators. But the South American *caimans* (**kay**-muhns) also belong to the alligator group.

All crocodilians live in similar places—where the water meets the land, and where the weather is warm. Most of them prefer to swim in freshwater. But some, like the saltwater crocodile, swim mostly in salt water.

AMERICAN CROCODILE
Crocodylus acutus

CHINESE ALLIGATOR
Alligator sinensis

NILE CROCODILE
Crocodylus niloticus

FALSE GHARIAL
Tomistoma schlegeli

MORELET'S CROCODILE
Crocodylus moreleti

BLACK CAIMAN
Melanosuchus niger

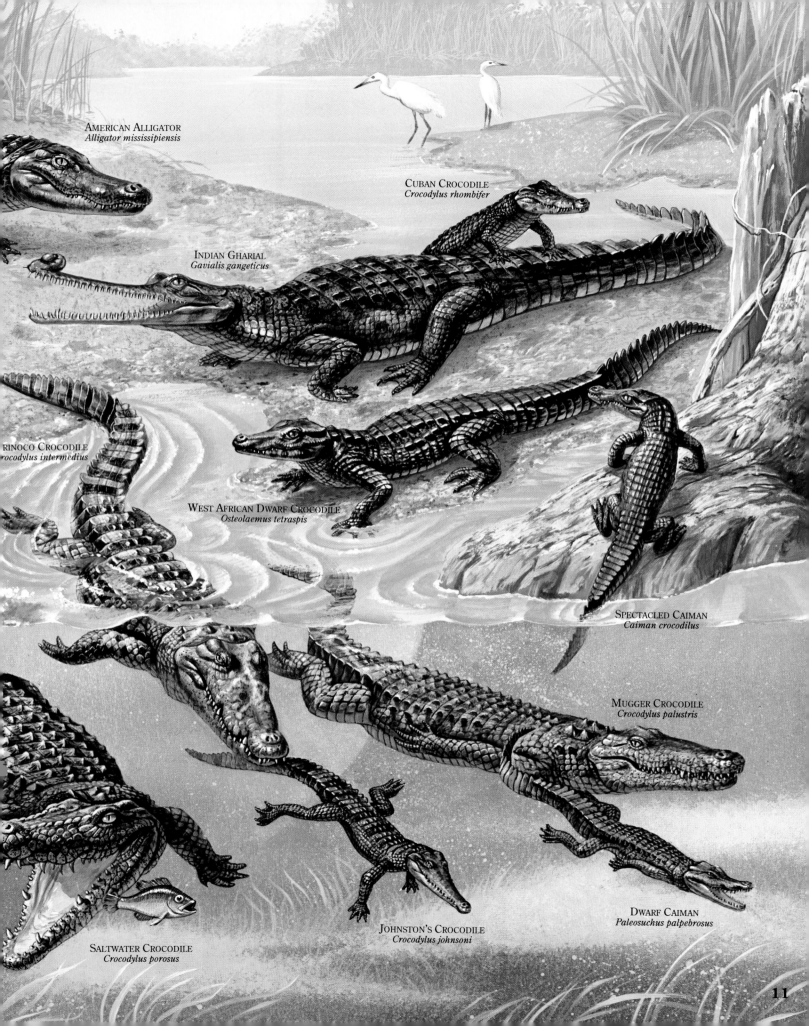

AMERICAN ALLIGATOR
Alligator mississipiensis

CUBAN CROCODILE
Crocodylus rhombifer

INDIAN GHARIAL
Gavialis gangeticus

RINOCO CROCODILE
rocodylus intermedius

WEST AFRICAN DWARF CROCODILE
Osteolaemus tetraspis

SPECTACLED CAIMAN
Caiman crocodilus

MUGGER CROCODILE
Crocodylus palustris

SALTWATER CROCODILE
Crocodylus porosus

JOHNSTON'S CROCODILE
Crocodylus johnsoni

DWARF CAIMAN
Paleosuchus palpebrosus

11

Dinosaurs and crocodilians were close relatives. In fact, they were both members of a large reptile group called the *archosaurs* (**ar**-kuh-sors), or "ruling reptiles."

While they lived, the dinosaurs were the most intelligent and advanced reptiles in the world. But 65 million years ago, they died out. Nobody knows why this happened, but it did. With the dinosaurs gone, the crocodilians are considered the most advanced reptiles left in the world.

TYRANNOSAURUS REX

STEGOSAURUS

ECHINODON

ALLIGATOR

If you think that some of the crocodiles living today are big, you should have seen some of their ancestors! The biggest living crocodilian is the saltwater crocodile, which can be almost 28 feet long. But 70 million years ago, there was a crocodile that may have been *50 feet long*! Scientists have named this huge animal *Phobosuchus* (foh-boh-soo-kuhss), which means "terrible crocodile." The head of Phobosuchus was six feet long, and it had teeth four inches long.

If you were alive 65 million years ago and had to guess which reptiles were going to survive—dinosaurs or crocodiles—you would have picked the dinosaurs. They looked much more successful. They had many different shapes, and they were able to live in many different kinds of places. But the crocodilians just kept living in rivers and swamps. And they always looked about the same. So it would have been a big surprise to learn that the crocodilians survived and the dinosaurs didn't.

Most reptiles have very small brains. But crocodilians have larger brains and are probably the most intelligent reptiles of all.

Like all reptiles, crocodilians are *cold-blooded* animals. This means that the temperature of a crocodilian's body depends on the temperature of the air and water around it. If it gets too cold, a crocodilian must find a way to warm itself. This is why crocodiles often bask in the hot sunlight ①.

1

②

PTERANODON

TRICERATOPS

NILE CROCODILE

When the air gets hot, crocodilians must find a way to cool off. One way to do this is to lie in the shade ②, where the hot sunlight won't hit them.

SPECTACLED CAIMAN

These reptiles can also cool themselves by holding their mouths open, just like a dog. As the moisture from their mouths evaporates, it cools them off. A crocodile can lie in the sun with its mouth open like this for hours.

During the day, crocodilians may go into the water to cool off, because the water is cooler than the air. At night, the water is usually warmer than the air, so crocodilians may go into the water to stay *warm*.

GHARIAL

CROCODILE

NORTH AMERICA

ASIA

AFRICA

SOUTH AMERICA

AUSTRALIA

CAIMAN

Around the world, crocodilians still live in the same places their ancestors did during the time of the dinosaurs *(green areas on map)*. They need to be in places where the water stays warm all year long. Only alligators can live in slightly cooler climates.

Crocodilians are fearless hunters. They will go after just about anything that comes near the water. And they are so strong that most animals are helpless against them. As soon as a crocodile manages to grab hold of its prey with its muscular jaws and pull it underwater, the animal is probably doomed.

But strength isn't the only thing that makes crocodilians excellent hunters. They are also very good at stalking their prey without being seen. They can often swim right up to another animal and grab it before it even knows they are there.

As a rule, crocodilians eat fish most of the time. But many adults also eat turtles, small mammals, and birds. And some, like the Nile crocodile, may attack very large mammals.

Most of the large animals that crocodilians catch are caught near the shore. The attack starts when a crocodilian sees an animal come down to the water to drink. The crocodilian dives quietly under the water. It swims toward the animal without being seen.

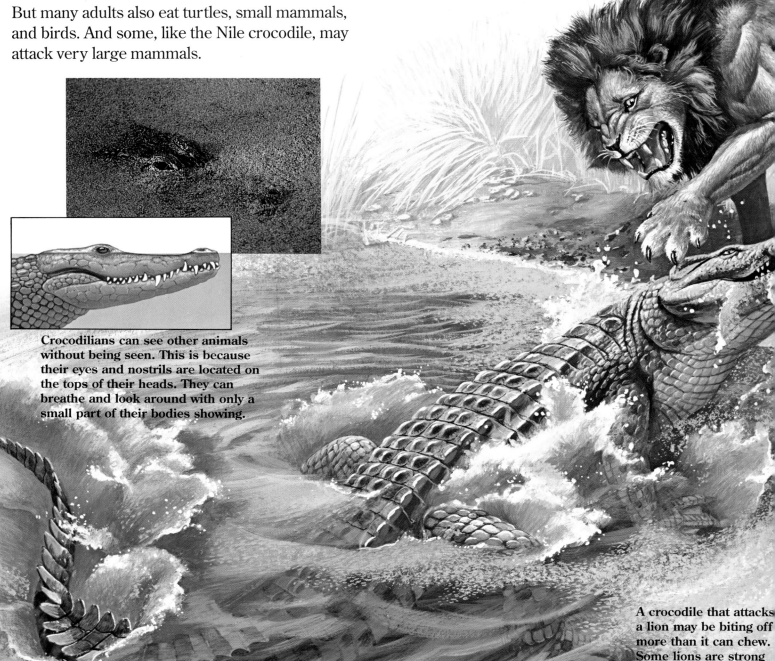

Crocodilians can see other animals without being seen. This is because their eyes and nostrils are located on the tops of their heads. They can breathe and look around with only a small part of their bodies showing.

A crocodile that attacks a lion may be biting off more than it can chew. Some lions are strong enough to win a fight with a crocodile.

When it gets close, it leaps out of the water and grabs its prey.

Crocodilians usually drag their prey back into the water and drown it.

WHITE-BREASTED CORMORANT

You might think that big animals like crocodiles would always be looking for food. But they really eat very little. In fact, this huge Nile crocodile eats about the same amount of food each day as the bird that's perching on its back. This is because cold-blooded animals don't need as much food to keep them going as warm-blooded birds and mammals do.

Crocodilians usually don't attack animals as large as lions. More often, they capture smaller prey, like the *capybara* (kap-uh-bair-uh) shown here. It is a favorite of the South American caimans.

CAPYBARA

IMPALA

Except for the hippopotamus, crocodiles are more dangerous to people than any other animal in Africa. People learn to be careful when they go to a stream to get water.

Impalas and other small antelopes are often taken by Nile crocodiles. The crocodile catches them by their feet as they drink from the river.

NILE CROCODILE

A Nile crocodile will eat almost anything. But it won't eat an Egyptian plover—not even when the bird walks right into the crocodile's mouth! This is because the birds sometimes pick the crocodile's teeth and help to keep its mouth clean.

Crocodilians are not fast runners. But they can leap out of the water so fast that their prey may not even see them coming.

17

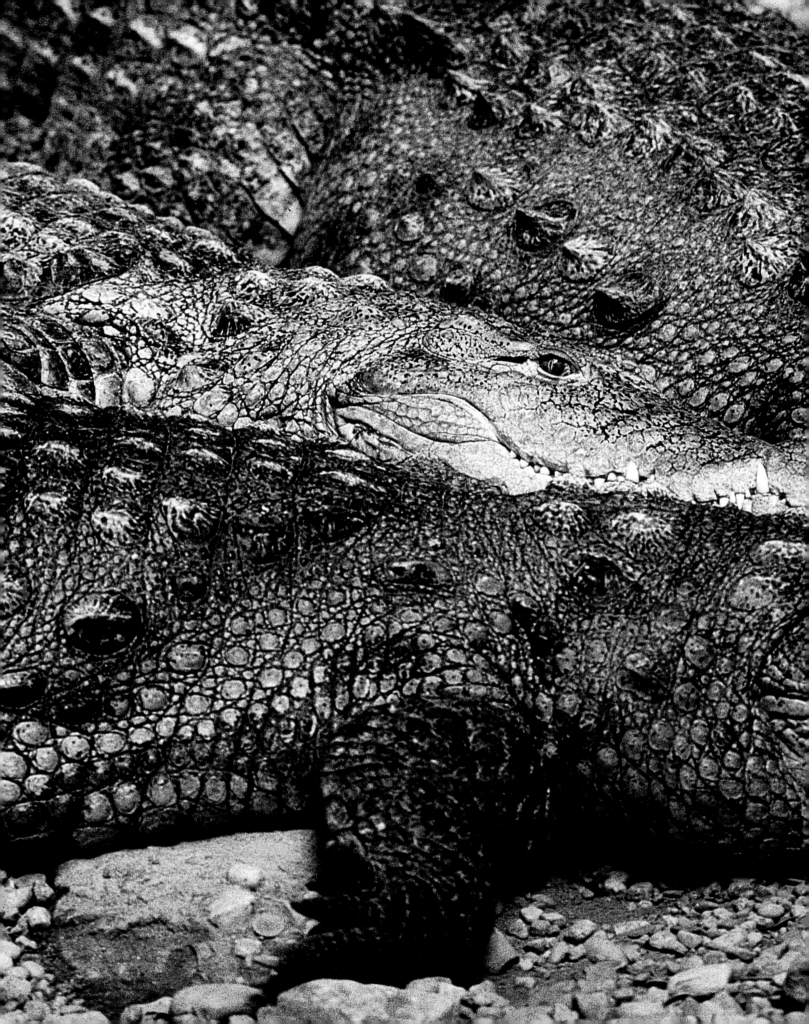

These marsh crocodiles live in India and Sri Lanka. How many animals can you find in the picture?

Crocodilian babies get better care from their mothers than you might expect. Most people think that all reptiles just lay their eggs and leave them to hatch on their own. But this isn't true of crocodilians. In fact, some crocodilian mothers can give their young a lot of protection—before they hatch, and for several months afterward.

It's a good thing, too, because baby crocodilians are born into a dangerous world. There are many animals that like to eat crocodilian eggs and the babies that hatch out of them. Without the protection that their mother gives them, all of the young would probably be eaten in no time. In some places, only one out of every 25 that hatch will grow up to become an adult.

There's no need for crocodilian mothers to feed their babies, because the young are able to catch their own food as soon as they hatch. But a crocodilian mother does many of the same things for her babies that other animal mothers do. The process begins when a female starts to build a nest, as shown at right.

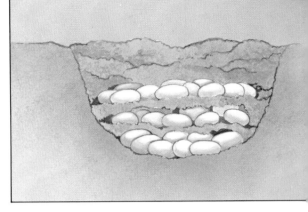

Crocodiles and alligators build different kinds of nests, but for the same purpose—to keep the eggs warm until they hatch. Most crocodiles dig a hole in the ground, as shown below. They lay up to 50 eggs in the hole, carefully arranging them in two or three layers. The eggs are then covered with sand to keep them warm. When the ground gets *too* hot the female will splash water on the nest or lay grass on top of it to keep it cool.

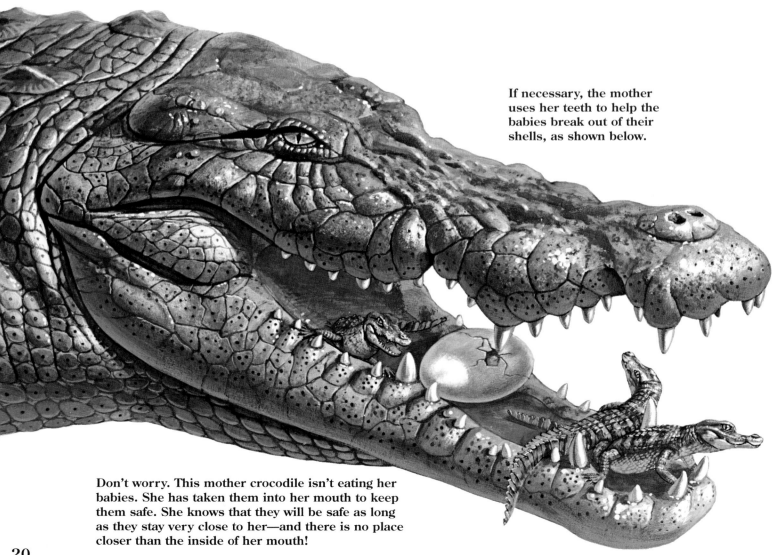

If necessary, the mother uses her teeth to help the babies break out of their shells, as shown below.

Don't worry. This mother crocodile isn't eating her babies. She has taken them into her mouth to keep them safe. She knows that they will be safe as long as they stay very close to her—and there is no place closer than the inside of her mouth!

Alligators build their nests *above* the ground. They make the nests out of leaves, branches and mud. After these materials have been gathered, the mother alligator shapes them into a mound about six feet wide and three feet high. She scoops out a hole in the center of the mound and lays 20 to 70 eggs in it. Then she covers it over. As the leaves and branches rot, they give off enough heat to keep the eggs warm.

Crocodile eggs are white and shiny. They are about three inches long, and they have very hard shells.

MONITOR LIZARD

Some large lizards and many small mammals like to eat crocodilian eggs. If the mother leaves her nest for even a short time, these animals may destroy all of the eggs before they can hatch.

Mother crocodilians usually stay near their nests to guard them. If any intruder comes close, the mother will drive them away.

AMERICAN ALLIGATOR

Young crocodilians have many enemies. Sometimes even the adult crocs like to eat them. For this reason, crocodilians spend the first two or three years of life hiding—until they grow big enough to protect themselves.

To help them break out of their shells, baby crocodilians have a pointed "egg tooth" on the tip of the nose. Soon after they hatch, the egg tooth drops off.

Like a duck with her ducklings, a mother crocodilian leads her young to the water. For the first few months of their lives, the babies may stay very close to the mother for protection. They even swim after her like baby ducks.

The future of alligators, crocodiles, and gharials is in human hands—and maybe on human feet as well. This is because the human desire for handbags, shoes, and other products made of crocodilian skins is the worst danger these animals face today. Unless people stop demanding these things, many species of crocodilians will soon be as extinct as the dinosaurs.

To satisfy the human demand for crocodilian skins, hunters have killed more than *20 million* alligators, crocodiles, and gharials in the last 50 years. All species have suffered from this, and some of the most beautiful have suffered the most. Saltwater crocodiles, gharials, and some species of South American caimans are now very close to extinction. How awful it is that animal species should die out just because they have beautiful skins!

Like all wild animals, crocodilians have also suffered because people are taking away or wrecking the places where they live. New roads, bridges, and dams frighten them away or keep them from swimming up and down rivers. In many places, people take land away from crocodilians to build houses on it—then they shoot the animals if they try to return to their former homes.

Fortunately, there are also people who are trying to save crocodilians. In some countries, land has been set aside where crocodilians can live in safety. Many governments have passed laws to control the amount of hunting. And some people have started to raise crocodilians on farms. The animals they raise are used to satisfy the demand for skins, and this may mean that fewer wild crocodilians will be killed.

Some people think that crocodilians should be allowed to keep their skins (and their lives). Others think that fancy handbags and shoes are more important. What do you think?

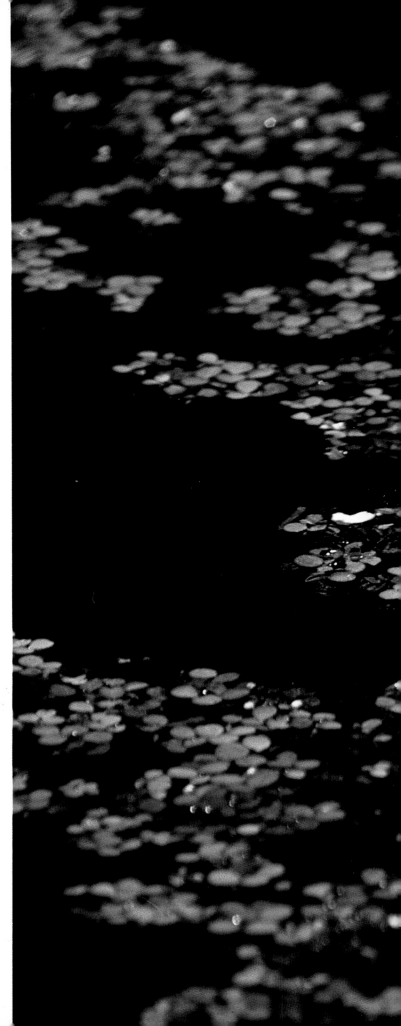

Index